# BELIEVE IT OR NOT!



## Shake a leg!

I'm Sparky the dog and I'd like to welcome you to *Believe it or not!* Prepare to be amazed by all the things you'll find out about in this exciting edition of *The Navigator*. On your journey through the pages you'll get icy with a scientist in Antarctica, and spicy with a wartime recipe for curried corned beef balls. You'll see a Saxon Hall through virtual reality glasses and you'll hear some ugly rumours about a Viking invasion. I'll even introduce you to some amazing insects.

**Just watch out for those pesky fleas!**

| Text Type | Literacy Skills | Wider Curriculum Links |
|---|---|---|
| Report | Interpreting visual information; deductive comprehension; inferential comprehension | **Geography** Unit 9: Village settlers **History** Unit 6B: Why have people invaded and settled Britain in the past? |
| Recount | Identifying differences between spoken and written language; distinguishing between fact and opinion | **History** Unit 6C: Why have people invaded and settled Britain in the past? |
| Explanation | Information retrieval; comparing information; exploring language of explanations | **Science** Unit 4C: Keeping warm |
| Discussion | Discursive and persuasive language; opinion; point of view | **Geography** Unit 8: Improving the environment |
| Report/ Instructional | Categorising information; advice versus propaganda; comparison of past and present language | **History** Unit 9: What was it like for children in the Second World War? |
| Recount | Close reading; summarising information | **Science** Unit 4A: Moving and growing |
| Newspaper: Recount | Skimming; distinguishing between fact and opinion | **PSHE:** Developing a healthy, safer lifestyle |
| Discussion/ Recount | Expressing and justifying an opinion; reflecting | **PSHE:** Developing confidence and responsibility |
| Explanation | Information retrieval; summarising information; linking text and visuals | |
| Report | Information retrieval; comparing information; deductive comprehension | |
| Fun spread | | |
| | | **ICT:** Year 4 Schemes of work |
| | | |

# Saxon Hall

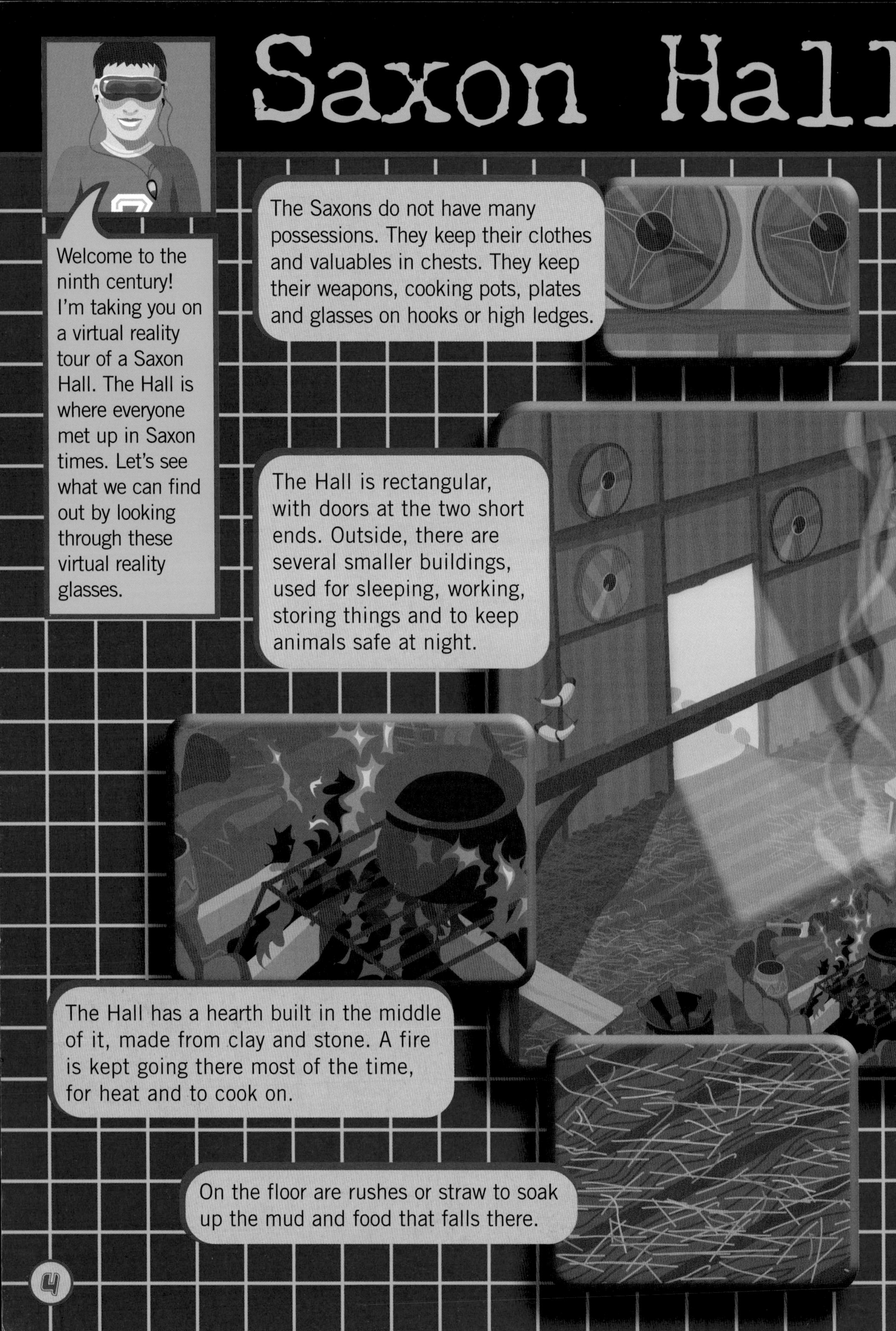

Welcome to the ninth century! I'm taking you on a virtual reality tour of a Saxon Hall. The Hall is where everyone met up in Saxon times. Let's see what we can find out by looking through these virtual reality glasses.

The Saxons do not have many possessions. They keep their clothes and valuables in chests. They keep their weapons, cooking pots, plates and glasses on hooks or high ledges.

The Hall is rectangular, with doors at the two short ends. Outside, there are several smaller buildings, used for sleeping, working, storing things and to keep animals safe at night.

The Hall has a hearth built in the middle of it, made from clay and stone. A fire is kept going there most of the time, for heat and to cook on.

On the floor are rushes or straw to soak up the mud and food that falls there.

# VIRTUAL TOUR

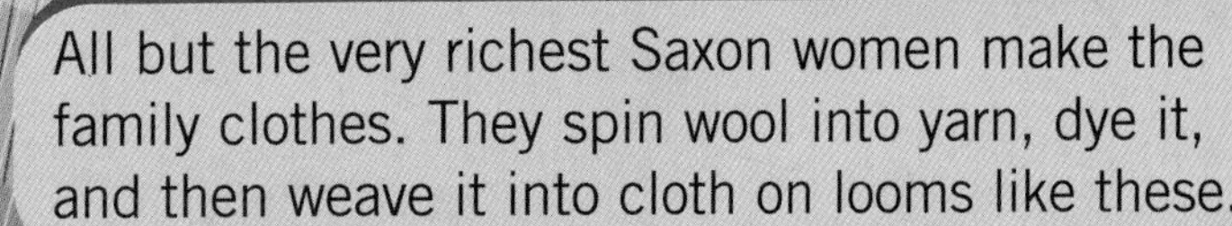

All but the very richest Saxon women make the family clothes. They spin wool into yarn, dye it, and then weave it into cloth on looms like these.

The roof is quite steep, so it is very high at the top. This means the smoke has plenty of space to drift up and out through the thatch.

The Saxons use wooden bowls, plates and spoons. They use glasses with rounded bottoms, which need a holder to keep them upright. The pottery is made by hand.

The people in this settlement grow or make all their own food. They grow corn for bread, beer and porridge. They keep animals for milk, eggs and meat.

Viking whispers
One day, in Anglo-Saxon times, a man was looking out to sea ...
This is about the time the Vikings raided last year. They stole my sheep. I wonder if that is a Viking longship?
I saw a ship out at sea. It could be Vikings. Perhaps they are coming to steal our sheep again.
Harold saw a Viking longship. It's a raid. They've come to steal all our sheep and corn again.

Viking warriors have landed!
They've come to kill us all!
People in the past, just like
people today, didn't always
pass on information correctly!

# A Message from

File Edit View Format Tools Actions Help

reply | print | delete | forward

From: Andy Wilkinson<a.wilkinson@basecamp.antarctica.com>
To: Sophie & Simon Wilkinson<wilkinsonfamily@coldmail.com>
Subject: Your school science project
Sent: Tues 1 June 2002 16:10:32

Hi Sophie and Simon

Many thanks for your message and attachments. The pictures taken with the new digital camera are great. I can't wait to get home and see you all for real!

Your science project sounds really interesting. We have to think all the time about heat loss and the temperature here in Antarctica, or we would soon freeze. At this time of year (don't forget it's the middle of winter here in June) the temperature can fall to –50°C. You need plenty of layers of thermal insulation to stop all your body heat escaping. I found labelled pictures of our standard outdoor gear and thermals. I've scanned them and attached them to this e-mail. Hope it's useful for your project.

Talking about thermal insulation set me thinking about the emperor penguins we've been studying. They are amazing birds. The males incubate the eggs for two months in the coldest part of winter, and don't eat during this time. They have thick layers of fat and soft feathers to insulate their bodies, and thousands of them huddle together for extra warmth. Each male holds a single egg in a warm, feathery pouch on top of its feet. I've attached a great picture I took last year at the emperor penguin colony. Hope you like it!

Love to you all
Dad
x

Penguins.jpg

Outdoor gear.jpg

Thermals.jpg

# the South Pole

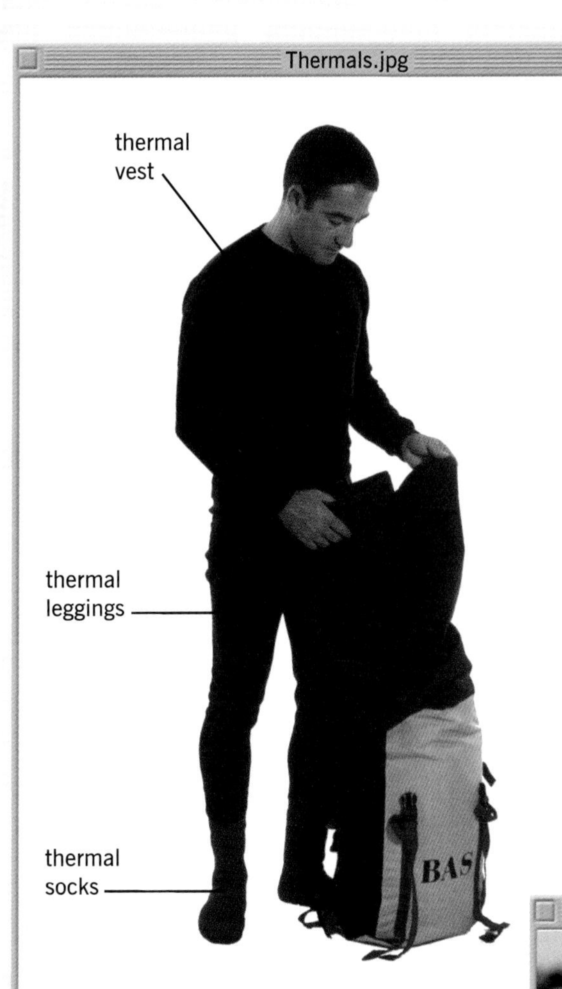

# WHAT A WASTE!

**What do you think about recycling? This web board gives some different views on what should happen to household waste. Who do you agree with? Who puts forward the best argument?**

From: fredharris@yahoo.co.uk
Subject: Recycling is dull! Wed 14/11/2002 18:36

I can't be bothered with recycling my rubbish. It takes too long to sort out the cans, newspapers and bottles and all of that. I have better things to do with my life. The local councils should deal with the rubbish – that's what we pay them for.

From: rosie01@hotmail.com
Subject: Re: Recycling is dull! Wed 14/11/2002 19:05

Recycling saves energy and reduces waste. Less waste means less countryside being dug up to bury the rubbish in and less pollution. Instead of having better things to do with your life, you should put a little time into making life better for everyone!

From: carl@hotmail.com
Subject: Re: Recycling is dull! Wed 14/11/2002 20:03

Here in Austria we recycle 50% of our household rubbish, just as they do in Germany, Switzerland and the Netherlands. This is five times better than you in Britain. You only recycle 9%. You should do better!

From: marielaurie@rsp.net
Subject: Re: Recycling is dull! Thurs 15/11/2002 17:45
Re-using saves even more energy and materials than recycling. I often buy clothes from the charity shop and we always keep plastic bags and jam jars to use again. We grow herbs in old yoghurt pots on the windowsills.

From: superchick2000@yahoo.co.uk
Subject: Re: Recycling is dull! Thurs 15/11/2002 18:56
Marie, you sound just like my mother! She has cupboards stuffed with plastic bags and jam jars, more than she can ever use. Making new things provides jobs and we all need those. Recycling centres and recycling bins are ugly. Get rid of them all, that's my opinion.

From: imran.s@miltonschool.net
Subject: Re: Recycling is dull! Thurs 15/11/2002 19:35
But recycling provides jobs too, just different jobs. And if you think recycling centres are ugly, have you never seen a landfill site, or a waste mountain? They are SO UGLY and they smell! Landfill pollutes the air with methane gas and it poisons the land. Maybe incinerators are better?

From: dscoleman@yahoo.com
Subject: Re: Recycling is dull! Fri 16/11/2002 16:50
Incinerators also pollute the air and they destroy all the materials that could be recycled and used again. But you're right, Imran – landfill sites are horrible. I know because I live near one. They smell and we get a lot of noise from the rubbish trucks driving there all the time. Litter blows off them and the sites are full of rats.

# THE KITCHEN FRONT

**DURING THE SECOND WORLD WAR, the government said that while soldiers fought on the War Front, those left behind fought too – on the Kitchen Front. Why did the government bother about cookery when there was a war on?**

- Ships that had carried food from other countries were needed for the war. People had to manage on home-grown food.
- Because there was less food from other countries, food had to be rationed – people could only buy set amounts of some foods. They had to manage with less food and less choice.
- People had to stay healthy. They had to eat food that was good for them. They also had to eat unfamiliar food, such as whale meat.

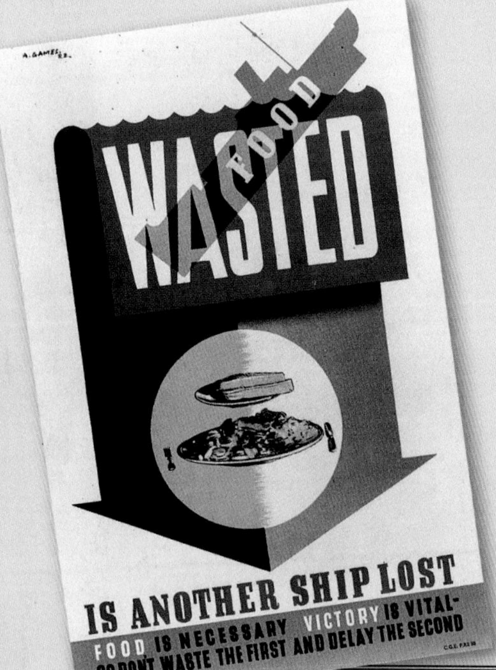


*People were encouraged to use ingredients that grew in the garden, such as potatoes, which were were not rationed. Recipe cards gave ways of cooking with potatoes in almost everything. The cards also explained how to use unfamiliar things, like dried egg powder. This was supposed, when mixed with water, to be just like fresh eggs. It wasn't!*

*Government propaganda told people that if they wasted food, they were helping the enemy. Any food left on your plate went in a 'pig bin' for local farmers to feed their pigs.*

The government found all sorts of ways to get their messages into newspapers.

## *A meaty subject...*

**She needs as much meat as he does!**

**Do manual workers need more meat?** No. Daily wear and tear on the tissues is not affected by the kind of work done.

## *Why is a potato like a lump of sugar?*

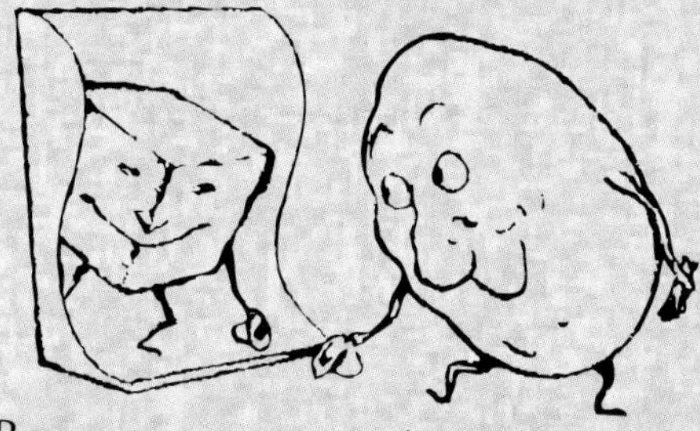

Because a potato and a lump of sugar are both turned by the digestive system into exactly the same thing – glucose – fuel which the body 'burns' to give energy and warmth.

Potatoes contain two important health protecting vitamins and a little body-building material of very good quality.

RECIPE OF THE WEEK

# Curried corned beef balls with mashed potato

Serves 4 people

1/2 oz fat
1 tablespoon grated onion
1 teaspoon curry powder
6 oz corned beef, chopped
1/2 teacup soft breadcrumbs
1/2 teacup crisp breadcrumbs
1/2 teaspoon Worcester sauce
a little milk
potatoes

**Method:** Heat the fat and fry the onion for 5 minutes. Stir in the curry powder and cook for two minutes, stirring well. Add the corned beef, the soft breadcrumbs and the Worcester sauce. Press into small balls, brush with milk and roll in the crisp breadcrumbs. Serve cold with plenty of mashed potato, or heat quickly under the grill or in the oven, if it is in use.

# A LIFE STORY IN ROCK

**What do a dead horse and a flat tyre have in common? Give up? They are two strange coincidences that led to the discovery of one of the most famous dinosaurs in the world today. Read on to learn about the amazing story of the huge Tyrannosaurus rex skeleton that was discovered in South Dakota, America in 1990.**

## THE FOSSIL HUNTERS

Susan Hendrikson was part of a team of fossil hunters who were looking for dinosaur bones on a farm in South Dakota, America. One day, the team found a dead horse on the farm. They found out that the horse belonged to Maurice Williams, a nearby farmer.

▲ *Sue was about the same size as a double-decker bus*

Susan Hendrikson with her amazing discovery

When Mr Williams came to collect the horse's body, the fossil hunters showed him around the dig site. Mr Williams told them that there were many rocky cliffs on his farm, which might contain dinosaur bones.

## AN AMAZING DISCOVERY

A few days later, the fossil hunters' truck got a flat tyre. Some members of the group took the truck into town to get the tyre mended. But Susan Hendrikson decided that she would walk over to Mr Williams' farm, to have a look around.

Susan looked closely at the cliffs on Mr Williams' farm. She saw a small pile of bones lying at the bottom of one of the cliffs. Wondering where they had come from, Susan looked up, and spotted something even more interesting. Three vertebrae (spine bones) and part of a femur (leg bone) were sticking out of the cliff!

## THIS IS ONE BIG ANIMAL!

Susan knew that these bones must have come from a very big animal. She took one of the bones back to the dig site, and showed them to the rest of the team. They all agreed that the bones came from the mighty Tyrannosaurus rex, the biggest dinosaur ever to have lived! They decided to call the T. rex 'Sue'.

The fossil hunters spent the next two years carefully removing all Sue's bones from the rock. They pieced the bones together to form Sue's skeleton, which is now on display at the Museum of Natural History in Chicago. Thanks to the hard work of Susan Hendrikson and the other fossil hunters, thousands of people can now see for themselves what a T. rex really looked like!

# FIT FOR KIDS!

By Michael Lawrence

● Olympic medallist Errol Derriere

**KIDFIT, the new children's fitness centre situated between the bingo hall and the prison, is open for business! Following months of hold-ups after the original contractors went bankrupt, KidFit finally opened its doors yesterday morning.**

Errol Derriere, Olympic Silver Decathlon Champion, was greeted warmly when he arrived to open the centre. As he cut the tape beside the heated indoor pool, Errol said, "I am thrilled to be here today. KidFit is a top-of-the-range sports facility. If there had been a local KidFit when I was at school, I'm sure I would have taken the Gold in the Olympics instead of the Silver. Great job, KidFit!"

Then, to wild applause, Errol took the hand of Mayoress, Margery Hunker, and they jumped into the pool.

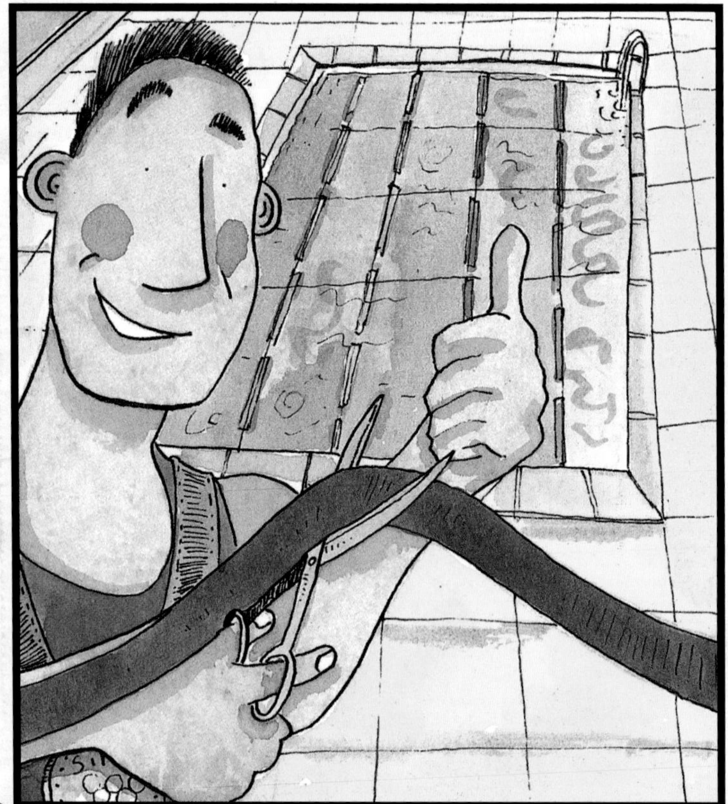

● Errol gives KidFit the thumbs-up.

● Errol causes a splash!

Unfortunately, in the excitement of the moment Errol had forgotten that he couldn't swim, but the Lady Mayor pulled him to the side by his hair and gave him the kiss of life. The Olympic champ was then given a nice cup of hot sweet tea to drink while he signed several autographs for fans.

KidFit's glossy brochure states that, "Children are the future. Getting fit and staying fit should be a fun experience for them. Our mission is to help today's children become tomorrow's healthy adults."

As well as the superb pool, the centre's facilities include an impressive array of exercise machines and an artificial rock-face for supervised climbing. There will be regular karate, Tai Kwon Do and kick-boxing sessions, plus training instruction in a variety of sports. For serious young sports people, there is an outdoor sports field that will be supervised at all times by semi-professional athletes. There is also a shop that sells sports clothing, equipment and novelty items such as sporty fridge magnets.

● KidFit's manager Del Runcorn

KidFit's manager, Del Runcorn, told this reporter, "This has been a very ambitious project, getting the centre from drawing board to opening day, but it was definitely worth all the time, money and effort. I am confident that the KidFit Children's Fitness Centre will be a roaring success."

The last word goes to eleven-year-old Dean O'Corke, one of KidFit's first members. Dean says of the centre, "Wow. Awesome. I'm gonna tell my mates about this place. Cool, really cool."

Yes, the last word about KidFit is "cool". Go check it out for yourselves, kids!

● KidFit member Dean O'Corke

# I WANNA BE

**Young people everywhere dream of becoming professional footballers. They long to win fame by playing the game that they love – and also be paid as much as £50,000 a week!**

## MAKING IT BIG

**Few kids break into the big time. There are many talented young players around, and not many places at clubs. The lucky few become apprentices at a club as soon as they leave school. The club looks after them in all sorts of ways. Firstly, it finds homes for them. Secondly, it makes sure that they follow healthy diets and train properly. Thirdly, it sends them to evening classes to continue their education.**

## DID YOU KNOW?

- *The youngest player to take part in the FA Cup was Andy Awford of Worcester City in 1987. He was 15 years and 88 days old.*
- *The youngest ever England International was Michael Owen, who made his debut against Chile in 1998, at the age of 18 years and 59 days.*
- *The most dramatic debut was made by 16-year-old Tommy Spratt in the 1957–58 season. Playing for Manchester United's fifth team, he scored 14 goals in a 25–0 victory!*

Michael Owen

# A FOOTBALLER!

## A DIFFICULT GOAL

But even very skilful players might not make it as professional footballers. Sometimes their growing bodies cannot cope with all the hard exercise. Sometimes they do not get on well with the manager and the other members of staff. And sometimes they have second thoughts about what they really want from life – as this story shows:

A small, shy 15-year-old arrived in Manchester from Northern Ireland. A scout had arranged for him to have a two-week trial with Manchester United. On the second day, he got so homesick that he went back home to Ireland, planning instead to become a printer's apprentice. But his father persuaded him to give football a try. So he did. Seven years later he scored one of the goals at Wembley when Manchester United won the European Cup Final, and he was named European Footballer of the Year. He was the brilliant George Best.

*George Best*

*This young boy grew up to be a famous footballer. Can you guess who? Check your answer with the one printed upside down at the bottom of the page.*

ANSWER: *David Beckham*

# Laughter is the best medicine

## CELL ME A JOKE!

When you see or hear something funny, you want to burst out laughing, and that benefits your health. Just what are some of these benefits? For a start, a good laugh helps your body to work well!

Your body is made up of trillions of cells. For example, the cells in your muscles help you move; cells in your nerves help you see, feel, touch, taste and hear; and cells in your bones stop you from falling down.

When your body is working well, the germs that can make you ill find it more difficult to attack you.

Defender cells help your body to fight the germs that find their way into your body through your mouth, nose or ears, or through a cut in your skin.

## ROUND AND ROUND

Did you know that when you laugh, you breathe out air at up to 70 miles an hour?

Laughing helps to bring oxygen into your blood, which the heart pumps round your body. As you catch your breath while laughing, you are taking lots of oxygen into your lungs. The heart sends blood to the lungs to collect this oxygen, before sending it to the rest of your body.

A good laugh makes you feel just great!

HA! HA! HA!

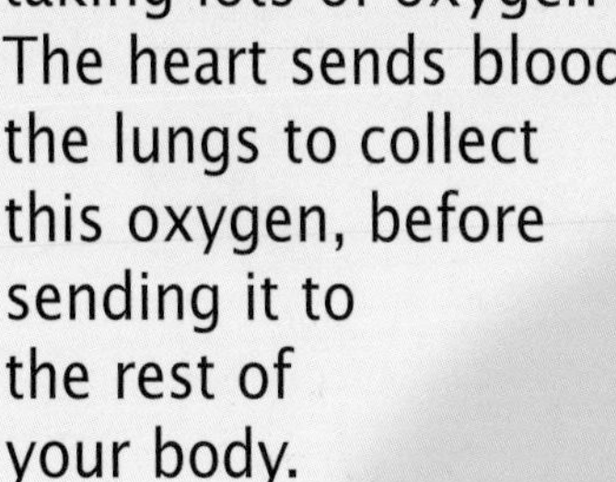

## They're both good for your health!

### NICE AND STEADY

Laughing also affects your blood pressure. Blood pressure is the pressure put on your arteries by the blood flowing through them. If your blood pressure is too high, you start to feel unwell – you can become tired, get headaches, and you may collapse. However, if it is too low, then not enough blood is pumping through your body. Laughter helps to keep your blood pressure at a healthy level.

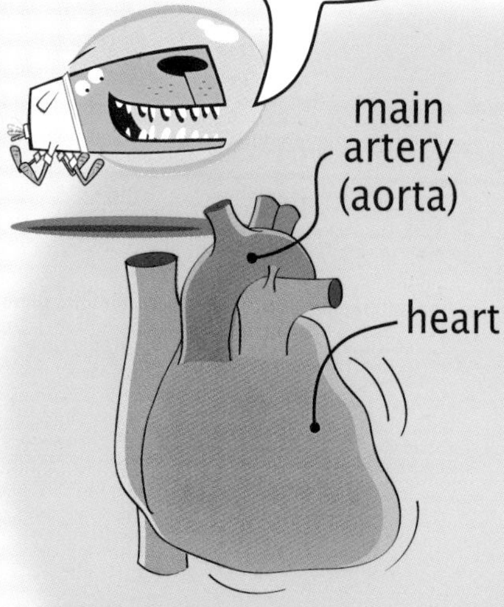
Arteries are the tubes that carry blood away from the heart to the rest of the body.
main artery (aorta)
heart

### BREATHE IN!

HA! HA! HA!

Laughing is great if you have asthma as it helps to improve your breathing. This is because when you laugh you take in more air than normal and your lungs gradually get bigger and bigger. This exercises your lungs and makes them stronger. All this breathing in and out while laughing is giving your respiratory system a good workout!

### TICKLED TO DEATH?

What happens when someone tickles us? We usually burst out laughing and beg for mercy! There is an explanation for this. The body's most ticklish areas, the armpits and the ribs, are the ones we automatically try to protect. So when we are tickled, our brains react by laughing, while our bodies pull away and want the tickling to stop.

## JUST FOR A LAUGH

***What do you get if you cross a dog with a giraffe?*** An animal that barks at low flying aircraft

***How do hedgehogs play leapfrog?*** Very, very carefully

***What goes dot dash ribbet?*** Morse toad

***What's green and scaly and red at the bottom?*** A dragon with nappy rash

***Why were the elephants thrown out of the swimming pool?*** Because they couldn't keep their trunks up

***How do you get five donkeys on a fire engine?*** Two in the front, two in the back and one on the top going EE-AW-EE-AW

# THE MUMMY'S TALE

**Most of us feel squeamish just thinking about mummies, so what makes some people study them? It's because mummies have interesting tales to tell. Studying them can tell us about food, clothes and tools of the past, and about ancient customs and beliefs.**

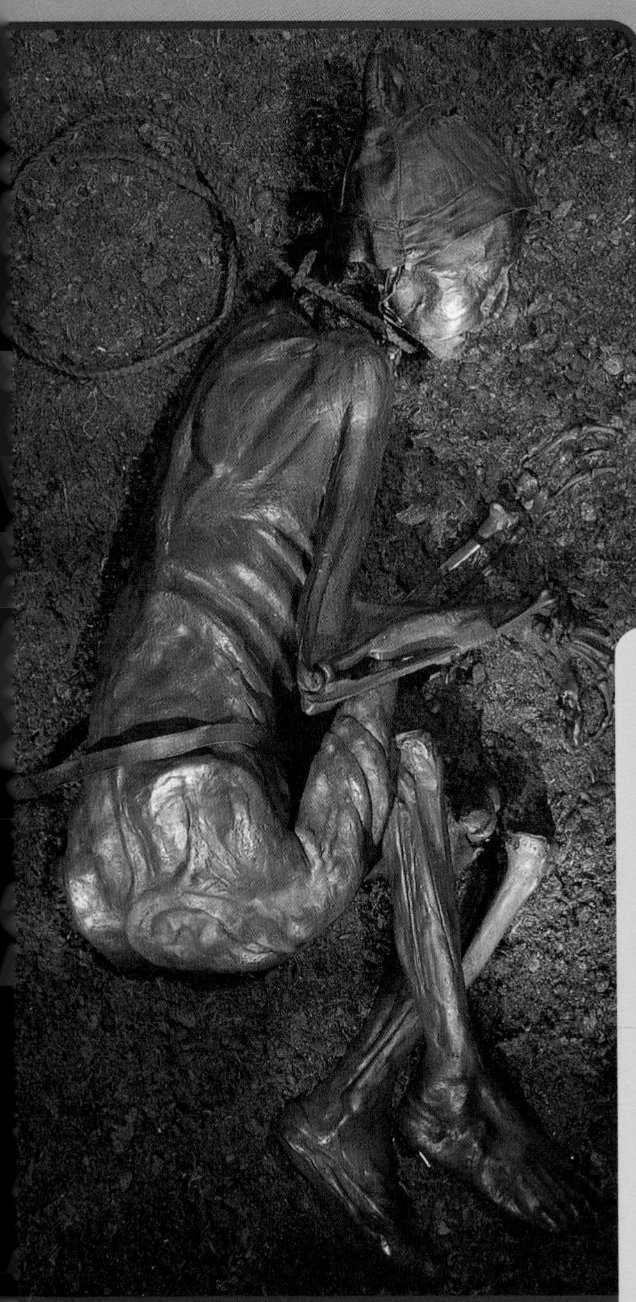

## *What is a mummy?*

A mummy is a dead body that has been preserved over hundreds or thousands of years. Some mummies are preserved on purpose by a special treatment called embalming. Others are preserved by accident; for example, because they froze soon after death.

## TOLLUND MAN

In 1950, a man's preserved body was found in a peatbog in Denmark. It was about 2000 years old. The man was wearing nothing but a leather cap tied under his chin, a belt around his waist and a noose around his neck. He had been hanged. On examining his stomach, scientists found that his last meal had been a thin porridge made from seeds and grains. They believe he was killed as a sacrifice to an Earth goddess.

## TUTANKHAMUN

In 1922, a British explorer discovered the tomb of Tutankhamun, a ruler of ancient Egypt. The 3000-year-old tomb contained not only the King's mummy, but also food and drink, board games, musical instruments, furniture, jewellery and other treasures. The Egyptians, who believed in an afterlife, had embalmed their king's body and provided these things for their king to enjoy.

## WOOLLY MAMMOTH

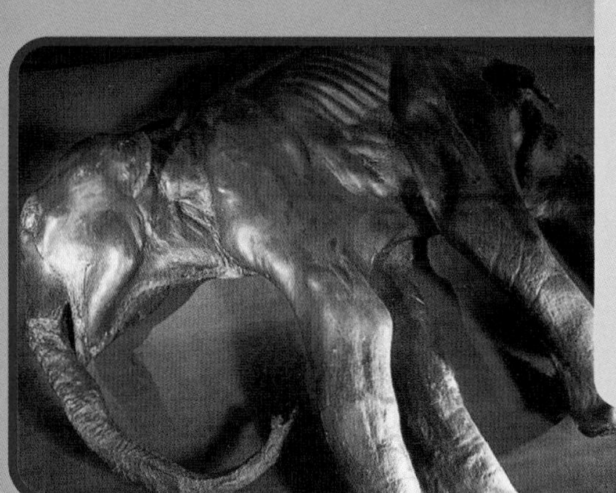

The frozen mummies of woolly mammoths are sometimes found in the Arctic ice. Mammoths became extinct about 11 000 years ago. Their frozen bodies have helped scientists to understand what the animals must have looked like. Mammoths were about three metres tall, and had huge curved tusks.

## INUIT MUMMIES

In 1972, the mummies of eight Inuit people – six women and two children – were found in a tomb in Greenland. They date from about 1475. The bodies had dried out naturally in the freezing Arctic air. They were wearing sealskin clothes to keep them warm, and high boots stuffed with grass. The stomach of one of the women contained the remains of seal, reindeer and hare.

# Insect INFO

***Love them or hate them, insects are all around us, and they were here way before the dinosaurs. There may be over 30 million species of insects (that's ten times more than all the other animal types put together!) and sometimes it feels like they all live in your house and garden!***

Here are a few things I bet you didn't know about these amazing little creatures!

## SPORTY TYPES

- Fleas can jump 30 cm – that's 130 times their own height!
- One type of cockroach can run 50 times its body length in one second!
- Scarab (dung) beetles can lift weights 850 times heavier than their own bodies!

## IT'S TOUGH ON THE OUTSIDE

Think what it would be like if you had to get rid of your skin every so often in order to grow! Insects have to do this. Their skin is called an exoskeleton. It's made of something called chitin, and it's light, waterproof and tough, but doesn't stretch much. (Ever wondered what that crunch was when you stepped on a beetle?) When an insect gets too big for its skin, it grows a new exoskeleton and sheds the old one.

## WHAT BIG EYES YOU HAVE!

Insects see with amazing compound eyes. Each compound eye is made up of hundreds of little eyes called eye-lets.

With all those eye-lets, insects have a very wide view. That's why it's so hard to splat a fly – it sees you coming as soon as you begin to move.

## ANTENNAE ANTICS

Imagine you could smell, touch, hear and talk – all with the same body part! Insects' antennae do all this.

- When an ant finds food, it uses the tip of its abdomen to squash some of the food and make a scented trail back to the nest. Other ants use their antennae to follow the scent to the food.
- Ants also tap their antennae together, like Morse code, to pass on information (for example, to warn other ants of danger).
- Insects living in groups, like honey bees, use their antennae to release an alarm scent to others when danger is near. When the danger is gone, they release a calm 'all-clear' scent.
- Have you ever been bitten by a mosquito? If so, was it at night? Mosquitoes use their antennae to detect heat. That means they can find us humans, even in the dark!

## WHAT'S IN A NAME?

- When it is alarmed, the bombardier beetle fires a hot, burning liquid from its rear and makes a 'pop' sound!
- The stag beetle has a pair of huge jaws that look like deer antlers. It uses these to fight other stag beetles by trying to grab the opponent's abdomen and flip it over onto its back.

- The female dung beetle rolls up a ball of dung, then pushes it to a safe spot and buries it. The beetle then lays eggs in the ball and uses it as food for itself and its grubs.

## I AM THE GREATEST!

- The longest insect is the giant stick insect from Borneo. These huge creatures grow to 33 cm long!

- The fastest flyer is an Australian dragonfly that can reach a speed of 58 mph!
- The heaviest is the Goliath beetle from Africa, which can weigh up to 100 grams!

# Byte-Sized ICT

## Viking whispers

### More whispering

Can you think of a rumour that might gradually change as it gets passed from one person to another? Often, things end up sounding more dramatic than they really are. Sometimes words are misheard and the meaning changes completely.

Have a go at creating your own cartoon, using clip-art. Your computer may have a 'speech bubble' tool, to allow you to type in the words that are spoken. Base your cartoon on another event in history. You could try to make it funny, if you like. Remember – before the invention of TV, radio, newspapers, telephones and the Internet, people had to tell each other the news face-to-face.

# A message from the South Pole

## Model for a day

Just what are you wearing? Ask a friend to take a picture of you wearing your school uniform, using a digital camera. Insert your photo into the publishing software on your computer and add some labels.

Now what? Well, why not ask your teacher how your picture could be used? If you are lucky, it could be printed out in colour and used on a display in your school entrance or in your school prospectus. You might even be able to put the picture on your school's website if you have one. You'd better make sure your uniform is looking smart, though!

# What a waste!

## Waste research challenge

Just how are we damaging the environment by not recycling? What can we do to change our ways? Use the Internet to find out more about waste and recycling.

You could try using a search engine to find useful sites. Remember to think of a few different words to search for, connected to the theme of waste. You could also try looking for the websites of environmental charities (charity websites usually have .org.uk at the end). Your local council's website might have section on what can be done in your area.

Using the websites you find, try to make a list of at least three things you can do to cause less waste.

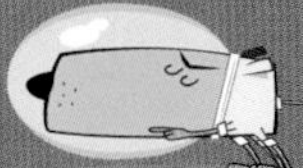

## The kitchen front

### Wartime food adverts

Could you have persuaded people to grow their own food during the Second World War? How would you get them to avoid throwing any food away? The government at the time tried to make people feel that they were helping the war effort by being careful with food and growing their own.

Use publishing software or a word-processor to have a go at designing an advert for a newspaper, encouraging people to grow their own food and not to waste it. Remember, in wartime it would be printed in black and white, so you will have to use font sizes and styles to make an impact – not colour!

Try to come up with a catchy saying or slogan too – one that will stick in people's minds. If you have a composing program on your computer,  you could also make up a tune to turn your saying into a jingle for the radio.

## Fit for kids!

### Read all about it!

What has happened in your school or class recently? Think of some headlines for any exciting or important events. Use a word-processor to type them out, making them look like a newspaper. You will need to use a font such as Times or Arial, which has with bold, capitals and large sizes.

Remember to keep your headlines short and snappy. Try to catch people's attention by making them sound dramatic. You could try to have a few words beginning with the same letter, such as 'School Secretary Slips on Snail'. Print them out and ask a friend to guess the event.

# Laughter is the best medicine

## It's a joke!

Get together with your mates and have everyone roaring with laughter! Type up your favourite jokes to make mini joke book or joke sheet. If you can, try including a picture for each one. Type the joke first, and then start a new page to type the punch-line. Make sure you use a nice cheery font in a fairly large size.

### Helpful hint!

On some word-processors you can press Ctrl + Enter on the keyboard to get a new page.

# Glossary

**afterlife** life after death. The Ancient Egyptians believed that when they died, they went on to another, everlasting life

**Anglo-Saxons** The people who invaded Britain from the Germanic part of Europe between the 5th and 7th centuries and settled

**Antarctica** the ice-covered continent surrounding the South Pole

**apprentice** someone who is learning his job and is taught by a particular employer for a fixed period of time

**decathlon** a two-day competition for men consisting of ten separate events

**embalming** preserving a body, originally by using spices

**eye-lets** small individual eyes that make up an insect's compound eye

**femur** the thigh bone

**fossil** the remains of a plant or animal preserved in the earth

**glucose** a type of sugar found in, for example, fruit and blood

**incinerator** apparatus for burning refuse to ashes

**incubate** to hatch eggs by keeping them warm

**Inuit** the people who live in the Arctic Lands of Greenland, Canada and Alaska

**jpg** a picture file sent as an attachment to a computer document

**longships** fast, strong ships used by the Vikings for raiding

**landfill** a large area of wasteland that is set aside to bury rubbish

**loom** apparatus for weaving yarn into fabric

**methane** a natural gas that has no smell

**mummy** a body preserved in Ancient Egypt through a process of drying, then being covered in powder, oils, resin, and wrapped in linen

**propaganda** information that is aimed at people in order to make them think and act in a certain way

**recycling** the process of turning household waste into material that can be re-used

**respiratory system** the lungs, airways, throat and nose make up the respiratory system

**vertebrae** the individual parts of the backbone

**Vikings** farmers, craftsmen and traders who lived in Norway, Sweden and Denmark in the Middle Ages. When they began to sail to raid other countries, the word Viking came to mean 'pirate'

**virtual reality** make-believe reality achieved through a certain sort of computer

**yarn** threads made by spinning and used for weaving, knitting, etc

# Index